MW00780438

Dear Christmas Mothers

The Legacy of Home Press
puritanlight@gmail.com

"Dear Christmas Mothers" copyright 2013 by Mrs. Connie
Hultquist, and Mrs. Sharon White.

All Rights Reserved.

No portion of this book may be copied without permission
from the publisher.

The Legacy of Home Press
ISBN-13: 978-0615901145
ISBN-10: 061590114X
Dear Christmas Mothers

Author - Mrs. Connie Hultquist
Compiled and Edited by – Mrs. Sharon White

Second Printing: April 2014

(Cover photo by Lynetta Hamm: Five of Connie's six grown
children.)

Dear Christmas Mothers

Dear Christmas Mothers

By Connie Hultquist

Contents

Dear Christmas Mothers

Dear Christmas Mothers

Introduction

Connie Hultquist, wife of almost 40 years to Jim, is the mother of six children and a grandmother of ten. She started writing letters to homemakers in 1996. These were handwritten newsletters and an encouragement to many.

Her first book, "*Dear Kitchen Saints*," was published earlier this year. It has become a best seller, and a blessing to many.

"*Dear Christmas Mothers*" is a compilation of 17 letters written to mothers.

These are from the years 2000 to 2005, during Thanksgiving and Christmas - time. We have gathered this holiday selection of her writings to inspire housewives to have an old fashioned Christmas.

These are printed here with a date by each letter. They are arranged in an organized fashion, but are not set up consecutively.

We've included a small recipe section of a few of Connie's favorite Christmas foods. We hope you enjoy this small volume.

May your family be greatly blessed this Christmas season!

- The Publisher, November 2013

1
An Old Time Christmas

November 14, 2005

This morning, as I was up praying, I was thinking "Wow! It won't be long until Christmas." Ya know, Papa and me raised 6 children and we love Christmas. I should be writing about Thanksgiving, as it is the next holiday. But if you have a large family, as Papa and me raised, you have to think of Christmas even in October.

We had to start early to gather presents for each of our children. Mary, our sixth baby, was just 8 months old for her first Christmas, and Jimmy was in the Navy. Well, I had to send Jimmy his present early to get it there in time for Christmas. I sent fudge and Christmas cookies to remind him of the tastes of home. Shoot, we never had a lot of money for Christmas presents. But we got what we could to make each of our

Dear Christmas Mothers

children feel special and loved by Daddy and Mama. We would give them one item of clothing like a warm sweatshirt. And then some kind of an inexpensive toy. In their stockings, we put candy and for the girls, hair ribbons or barrettes. And for the boys always basketball cards. I hear the little boys' childhood voices as I write. "Daddy, you are lucky — you pick out the best cards. You always get the good ones." Dan said he didn't know what he wanted to be when he grew up, but he knew he would be in the NBA. Like it was a done deal. But we started packing little toys and fun things away in October to surprise the children for Christmas Day.

   The children would have us take them to the Dollar Store to buy a dollar gift for each of the members of their family. They each had their own money, as they did a once a week paper route. So when David and Mary and Dan were little, and the other children were grown, we took the 3 youngest to the Dollar Store. So the 3 children represented 30 bucks, and all of them wanted me to help pick out presents. I was about cross eyed by the time I helped pick out 30 - one dollar presents. And yet now, 15 years later, I would jump at the chance to do that all over again.

And ya know, somehow each year, we got a real Christmas tree for the family. We would find one for about 10 bucks. And, oh, the children's hands would just tremble with excitement as they put the first ornaments on the tree. It was a special night to behold. I would fix chili and cornbread. And after supper, we would decorate the tree. Papa was so full of fun and loved Christmas. I tried to have some Christmas cookies made for the evening and always popcorn. After the tree was all decorated, our dog Daisey would go sit under it. One time her collar got hooked to the tree and she knocked it over, and then as we all screamed, she ran away dragging the decorated tree through the house.

One year, Mary gave me such a precious gift. She didn't have any money of her own to spend for Christmas. She was just a wee little girl about 5 years old. Anyway, I had a precious old fashioned book that I had lost in the house someplace and couldn't find it for about a year. I

Dear Christmas Mothers

had finally given up ever trying to find it. Well about a week before Christmas, Mary found it upstairs, stacked in with some other forgotten books. And so for Christmas Day, she wrapped this book up for me and put it under the tree with a card that said "To Mom, From Mary." She has the same heart as I have and loves writing and books. So she knew how much Mama missed her book. So it was one of my favorite Christmas presents that year. I was so surprised to see it again, as I thought it was lost forever. And Mary was so proud of her little Christmas self.

   If you saw this book, you would weep. It is real old fashioned from the 1800's with a little girl about 5 on the front cover. She is praying to Jesus. And inside the book are her prayers.

   Just after Thanksgiving, I would start my baking. Then about a week before Christmas, I would make simple coffeecakes to give to the neighbor families. I would have one of the children dress up warm and deliver a few cakes to the neighbors. I would make a few a day and when they were done, they were delivered. They were made simply. I would make up a huge batch

Dear Christmas Mothers

of sweet yeast raise dough. Then I would braid the dough for each cake and put it in a circle. I would put cinnamon and sugar on the braids before I wound them together. Then after they baked, I would put a light white powdered sugar glaze; then, on the top, green candy sprinkles. Then maybe red hots to look like berries on a wreath. Sometimes I put maraschino cherries on it, like in clusters of three. You can also add raisins to your sweet dough.

I would make about three Christmas cakes out of a batch of sweet dough. Then I would put the coffeecake on a pretty paper Christmas plate, and then put plastic wrap over it with a bow and a simple card "From the Hultquists. Merry Christmas." I loved doing this to teach the children to love and respect our neighbors and to teach them the Joy of giving. Of course, the neighbors would ooh and aahh and kid the children about "if they were naughty or nice and what was Santa gonna bring 'em for Christmas?" And when they would come back home, I would say, "Well, what did Chuck and Trudy say? Did they like the cake?" And the children would tell me what they said. It was a lot of fun. I look forward to having my grandchildren do this too, of course, when they are older.

I told Papa last week. "Thank God this Christmas we will have the grandbabies with us over the season, at least." I was reading to Baby Rose and showing her a Christmas book Papa had gotten for her. It had a Christmas tree. I explained to Baby that we would buy a tree, too. And I told her it would be for Grandma and Grandpa's house and she said, "And for ME?" And I said, "Oh, yes, Baby, for you, too."

We make a Christmas with our hands and with our hearts. Remembering that it is a time for Joy and a time to rest and enjoy the family. We must have hearts of trust in God in order to encourage our children and, by our behavior, excite courage in their souls.

And, ya know, as a young mom, I didn't want to make a Christmas, as I wanted to just celebrate Jesus' birth. But to tell poor children that we would have no Christmas as the other children had, and would only celebrate the birth of Christ, was not showing our children the love of Jesus and their parents' love. We celebrated both. And we let our children know that Jesus Christ was real but Santa was pretend, and we talked about Santa just to have fun.

And I bet I could say in my years as a wife and mother I have, without exaggeration, made at least a million cut-out sugar cookies. Maybe more! This is another dough for Mother to learn to work with. I would say sugar cookie dough is like noodle dough. These cookies were a mainstay for me at Christmas. Many years, I sold them to buy Christmas presents. Mary, at 9 years old, made these and sold 40 dozen to buy Christmas presents.

{Please see the recipe section on page 111 for sugar cookies.}

2
Dreams and Visions
November 21, 2005

Good Morning, Thanksgiving Mothers. Is everyone gettin' ready for Turkey Day? Today Mary and Jim and I will go to my Mom's to help her get the house ready for the family to gather on Thursday. My mom is 82 and will bake the turkey and have the celebration at her house. Of course, everyone helps and brings food. I will bring candied sweet potatoes and pies. Then each of the families will bring vegetable casseroles and salads.

I am having a sort of vision of an old time Thanksgiving. It must have been a Thanksgiving I went to as a child. I was about 3 yrs old. I remember the floor being covered with the old time carpet rugs. I see a warm fire as it glows. The floor is not even and you walk up and over the sagging floor. I can feel the humps under my feet as I write. And yet the Mother there in charge keeps a warm home.

The old carpet is pieced and tacked down. Ya know, the old timers would just patch a floor. Sometimes they would take a tin can and flatten it with a hammer. Usually it was a tobacco can, as they were flat. They split it apart and then would hammer it flat. Then they would put it over a hole in the floor and nail it down. Then the carpet went over that. The patches kept the critters out, too. Well, at least in the winter, they used carpet. Folks, ya know, just made do. They patched their carpet, just like they would their clothing, and they would just nail the pieces down with carpet tacks.

Anyway, as I walk on this floor with the patched carpet, I can feel the tin can patches under the carpet. They kinda squeak up and down under my feet. The house is sealed shut and a warm fire is blazing. It is evening and we just got there the day before Thanksgiving. We were expected earlier in the day but the snow storm kept us behind in time. So when we got to the farmhouse, the fire in the fireplace had been made and remade, and the fire was an even heat now in the house, and such a joyful fire it was.

All of us children laughed and teased each other until it was time to go to bed. I remember the uncles kidding us children, and the aunts were always more sober with the business of Thanksgiving at hand. The men would tease the women about being so worried about Thanksgiving and having everything just right.

I must be seeing an old farmhouse in the 40's. Because the carpet I see is about that era. And on the door is this heavy brown paper tacked over the whole door. The house is snug with much of the plastic paper on the outside windows and doors. As the wind whips in the cold, the sound of the brown paper on the kitchen door claps for the winter wind.

The country folks back in the early days were always less sophisticated than the city folks. They worried more about a warm home than the latest city styles. I used to hear them answer their city relatives with, "Oh, that's just for city folks." The simple folks out on the land were more common sense people who lived close to home. They namcd all of their animals and saw more of animals than of people.

Last night as I prayed, I said "Oh, Lord, who was supposed to be the older Titus mother in my life?" I longed for her to come to me and to just sit with me. I longed to see her face. Just once to see her face. I wrestled in prayer to see her face and I never did. And the Lord said to me, "Connie, just sense her presence."

I feel so bare boned and cold lately. So alone and not comforted. I may feel alone and, yet, the Lord shows me a country farmhouse with a patched floor and a warm fire to sit by. The wind howls outside, but inside the Lord's heart and place for me, it is warm and all of my needs are met there.

As a child growin' up in the 1950's — oh, we had the most wonderful Thanksgivings. The baked turkeys and hams, sliced thinly and so tempting. The children were always trying to steal a piece of meat before it was put on the table. The dinner was promised to be served at noon. But we were always waiting for some relative that was late. The women would look out the window and worry about "Aunt Whoever." And wonder and worry over them being late. No one made a long distance phone call to see if someone was on their way. I mean, you didn't call long distance unless someone died. Well, almost. And everyone yelled into the phone because it was long distance.

I remember as a child being in bed in the early morning and Mom calling her brother Clarence. Everyone called early in the morning, as it was cheaper to call. So Mom woke me up yelling "Clarence" into the phone. We children would scramble out of bed to see what disaster had happened as it was a long distance call! And ya only talked a minute as it was such a big deal and no one would dare talk loooong. So us kids knew something was really up and the call would be short. So we leaped out of bed to hear what our Mother was gonna say to Clarence. Sometimes it was just a friendly call about family. But always an emergency.

Sometimes the dinner would be heated again and again until everyone arrived around 2:00 in the afternoon. Finally we children would hear the cars rollin' in and we would announce, as we looked out the front window, "They're here! They're here!" Then we would yell who it was. "Can we eat now?" we would ask.

"Now, you kids just wait until everyone gets in and gets their coats off and gets settled, and then we will eat," our mothers always had to get after us.

Often Mother worried she didn't make enough food and then all the relatives brought food galore. "Oh, you brought a pumpkin pie?" Mom would say, as she helped the aunts off with their coats. "Oh, I was afraid we wouldn't have enough pie." And, oh, what glorious dinners the women made. Oh, mercy!   Several kinds of stuffings. Aunt Lilly wouldn't eat a thing with an onion in it. So Mom always made Lilly's dressing separate. But, oh, the fruit salads with the whipped cream were heavenly. My Dad had to have the old-fashioned cooked cranberry sauce. Nothing with oranges in it. No new recipes for cranberry sauce made him happy. My one aunt always made a salad with a secret salad dressing on it. She never gave us the recipe and, the whole dinner, the ladies would taste this dressing and try to guess what was in it. It tasted like the Dorothy Lynch dressing. But, oh, we would have loads of mashed potatoes and gravy and many vegetable casseroles.

And everyone was welcome. If someone didn't have a place to go for Thanksgiving, then they were welcome to ours.

One thing the women never made in my extended family was bread. None of the women ever brought bread of any kind to a Thanksgiving dinner. The women said they didn't need it with all the other good food. But, anyway, the standing joke with Dad was, when we were all ready to eat this wonderful feast, Dad would say, "Velma, where's the bread?" And Mom would get out her little bread plate and put it on the table and put a stack of white store bread on it.

And, oh, everyone would eat this heavenly food until they would burst. And after everyone left, just before supper around 5:00, my dad would say, "Velma, when is supper?"

And Mom would say, "Fran, how can you be hungry? We just ate all that food!"

Dear Christmas Mothers

I mean, we would eat desserts galore, too. Everyone was stuffed to the gillards.

But, too, when my family would arrive home and around 5:00 in the evening, Jim and the kids would ask me if we were gonna have supper. My family was always thin too but always ate at regular times. Back then, you didn't eat a lot of snacks. You just ate 3 meals a day. I mean, except on Thanksgiving, and you ate at dinner and then steady until you went back home.

And, oh, back at the old time Thanksgivings, the men couldn't wait to get a piece of pie. The cakes and apple crisps were passed over. The pies were the crowning glories of the Thanksgiving feasts. Pumpkin pie was the favorite but other pies would do. And when the pies were gone, then the other desserts were eaten.

And Mother was so giving and told folks to take leftovers home to their families. But Dad would whisper to Mom, "Don't give away the pie!" My Dad loved pie and you would be in serious trouble if you got in between him and his pie.

Dear Christmas Mothers

Often, if I brought a pie, I would leave Dad about a half the pie to eat later.

My pies, when the children were growing up, were terrible. But everyone ate them, anyway, as they all loved pie. Of course, with my pies, they just ate the inside and left the crust. They didn't want to break their teeth off. I can make pies now and I will bring them to Mom's dinner on Thanksgiving.

My milkman, "Dick," many years ago told me of an old family recipe for pumpkin pie. He said the old time Mothers would take a raw pumpkin and slice it up and pile it high in the crusted pie plate. Then over the top, they would put a handful of flour and cinnamon and brown sugar, and a bit of butter. Then they would put the pie crust on the top, put slits in the crust, and bake the pie. It would be like an apple pie. It sounds delicious to me and I may try that. I made a zucchini pie like this one year and it tasted exactly like an apple pie. I think I added a bit of vinegar or lemon juice to it to give it a twang.

Dear Christmas Mothers

But, pies! Pies, ladies! Make a pie for Thanksgiving for the men in your life. They will love ya for it.

3
Good Mothers and Happy Homes

November 24, 2005

I am up writing this morning and trying to clean a bit before Jim gets up for work.

We had a wonderful Thanksgiving. When we got home last evening, I didn't put all my stuff away. There is so much work on Thanksgiving to do that I hardly know if I ate anything or not. What with playing with the grandbabies and helping Mom with dinner, I didn't have much time to eat. I am there mainly to help and to give others a nice Thanksgiving memory. The old time mothers were like that. They helped the old folks fill their plates and kept the children occupied and happy. And afterward, they did the dishes.

When I was young, all the old aunts about me helped me with my children and now it is my turn. As a young mom, I would see all the aunts and mothers working to make sure everyone got

Dear Christmas Mothers

a full plate. We would all say to each of these working mothers, "Did you get a plate?" and they would say, "Oh, yes, I will eat as soon as I can get around." Meaning as soon as they knew everyone else had what they needed. The old folks need help, ya know. And the children need to be whispered to, "to be good."

After the coast was clear yesterday, I went down to the basement to play the piano. Romeo, age 3, played the bottom notes and Baby Rose, age 2, played the top notes. And Grandma played the middle part as I kept the children balanced on the piano stool.

And the night before Thanksgiving, I was so sick in the night. I couldn't hardly stand up without weaving. I didn't tell anyone. But I am here to tell ya that God healed me – oh, yes, He did. The next morning, I was healed. Well, ya know, I knew if I was sick, I couldn't give anyone a nice Thanksgiving. My Mother worked so hard, at age 82, to open her home to all of us. Jim and I went over midweek to help clean, then we all clean up before we leave. But Mom did a lot of work and the family needed a nice holiday of

Dear Christmas Mothers

memories. And, ya know, someday the kids will remember these happy times. They are rare times to teach the children and their parents sacrifice and a sense of duty. Oh, yes, I could weep and turn inward as I would like to do. But I think to myself, "Don't be a big baby, Connie, you have folks counting on you."

And, ya know, if you see a family that has generations of brokenness, you see a family who never had good mothers. Sometimes you see decent women in the family but they won't take any authority against the evil. They let things go on that they should have been praying over.

In some families, the older mothers are like babies — they never grow up. They won't take any authority to have a big meal and invite the family. They feel inadequate, I guess. But you always wonder about these families like, "Who is running this show, anyway?" So many of these mothers give outside jobs top priority. It takes their strength and dignity.

4
A Snowy Morning

December 2, 2000

Dear Christmas Ladies, It snowed just a little the other morning. But last night it really snowed. As I look out my window as I write, I see the fluffy white glistening snow. The great equalizer. Now my messy yard is hidden and it looks like everyone else's.

My lights sparkle in the window and the old fashioned candles stand awaiting Christmas.

Early this morning before Jim got up, I straightened everything and made it look pretty for him. I like to send him off to work with a joyful flavor of Christmas. I have a little angel lamp next to the manger scene. I try to have it all turned on when he gets up. Then, of course, the table is set with a Christmas candle.

Yesterday I fixed chili for supper and our little neighbor girl Heather, age 8, stopped to visit. I fixed elephant ears to go with our soup. I had been busy with Christmas things yesterday and I didn't have the bread ready for supper, so I made elephant ears. I invited Heather for supper.

"Are those ears from a real elephant?" she asked me.

Of course, I wanted to say "Yes" and see how big of a story I could get away with. But, being in such a big hurry to get supper on, I refrained and told the truth. "No, Heather, they are just made from bread dough."

Later on, after supper, I walked Heather home. "Connie, wait. Can you tell my Dad how to make elephant ears?" So I told him my recipe.

It is very easy. When you are making your yeast raise bread? ... and you need some bread for supper in a hurry? ... this is what you do.

Just take a wad of dough about the size of a dinner roll. Take your rolling pin and roll it out paper thin on a floured surface ... so it looks like a large pancake. Then fry it on a hot griddle or frying pan, like you do pancakes. They blister and bubble and are so tasty with hot soup. We butter ours while hot and sprinkle Parmesan cheese on the top. Or for a quick dessert,

Dear Christmas Mothers

sprinkle cinnamon and sugar on it. Mary and Heather had them both ways last night.

Then after supper I made a coffee cake with the rest of the dough. I just put a thin layer of dough in a pan and sprinkled it with cinnamon and sugar. Then I put another layer on the top and sprinkled that with cinnamon and sugar. I let it rise; then I baked it. Jim ate a lot of that as soon as it was out of the oven. I was surprised he did after eating that big elephant ear and several bowls of chili.

Dear Christmas Mothers

5
A Christmas Home

December 2, 2003

I am up brewing coffee. Just went to let the cat out this morning and he didn't even want to go. It's snowing with a cold wind blowing. Kitty is sitting by the door contemplating. He wants to go out but just ain't quite sure of it. After Papa wakes up this morning, we will be putting up our Christmas tree, but first I wanted to share some Christmas craft ideas with you Mothers on this early, quiet winter morning.

I have this large, old green basket that I use especially at Christmas. I set it out on the buffet and put packages of hot drink mixes in it. At one side, I may put out a jar of homemade cocoa mix, or a jar with herbs for tea, or just tea bags in a cute jar. I decorate any jar. Just save all of your little pickle jars or mayonnaise glass jars, clean off the labels, and then decorate them up with red ribbons — or maybe paste the front of an old

Christmas card on the front.

It's fun for friends and family when they come to your house to visit and mix up a hot drink. Our kids loved the hot cocoa mix. I usually made that in a gallon jar. They would invite a friend over and would mix their own hot cocoa.

One thing I love to make for a coffee creamer is this. Just take a jar and put in some of that Creamora, or some store brand of dry instant cream, and to this, add a package of the vanilla instant pudding mix. Like to two cups of Creamora, add one pudding mix, more or less. This makes a vanilla sugar. Or you could add a butterscotch instant pudding mix.

In the old days at Christmas, we Christmas sisters would buy a few vanilla beans and put these in our cocoa mix or in our sugar for holiday baking. But, mercy! Those vanilla beans cost about three bucks for one now. They can forget that. We used to get them two for a buck, I think.

But, anyway, just find an old basket and fill it with Christmas cheer. And beside your basket, set out some Christmas mugs. Ya know, if you are low on baskets, the Salvation Army has loads

Dear Christmas Mothers

of them and they are cheap. I just wash mine out with soap and water. Turn it upside down and let them dry over the hot air furnace vent. Also, in your basket, you could put some paper napkins, along with the hot drink mixes. And maybe a jar with the little marshmallows for the cocoa mix.

I just make my cocoa mix by how it looks. I make the flavored coffees, too. But I just make them by inspiration. I take the instant coffee and add brown sugar and dried cream, and put this in a jar for anyone who likes it like this. You could put in the pudding mix, too. For a mocha mix, just add cocoa to the instant coffee and sugar and cream.

Maybe you could line your holiday basket with a cute Christmas towel from the Dollar Tree. They just cost a buck. I got one yesterday and Papa bought me one, too, when I wasn't looking. He usually buys me a Christmas coffee mug each year, too. I mean all this stuff is dirt cheap at the Dollar Store. You can't hardly afford not to buy this stuff, and it all adds a Christmas cheer to the family home.

Also, you can make your own potpourri for the

Christmas fireside jars. Just take orange peels or lemon or lime or grapefruit peels and cut them up with your scissors, in strips. Put them in a favorite old-fashioned pan or crock bowl, or a bucket ... whatever. Anyway, mix this up with some pine cones from under your pine tree or your neighbor's pine tree. Mix in some cheap cinnamon sticks and whole cloves, bay leaves and whatever. Maybe add some old dry sticks from outside, or nuts in a shell. Just stir this all up. The peels will dry in the pine cones. Stir all this around every day, and it will all dry. If you wanted to, you could buy some scented oil at the Dollar Store to put in it. And then, to this mix, string the white Dollar Store lights.

Another thing I do during the Christmas season and well, all winter long, is this. I always have my big 2 gallon coffee pot on the stove with water in it to keep the air moist. This is a huge old fashioned white enamel coffee pot. Papa got it for me many years ago in a junk pile. It is a favorite kitchen pot. It has a bale handle and a handle at the side to hang on to. It's a handle at the bottom; it goes from side to side — like to hold in the palm of your hand and give you some leverage.

Anyway, to this simmering pot, I add each day an old bottle of spice of some kind out of my spice cabinet. This keeps my spice cabinet cleaned out and the house smelling spicy. You shouldn't keep your spices for year after year. They get old and this is one way to get rid of them without feeling wasteful. My aunt gave me some spices that she probably kept for 40 years, just using them on the holidays. Well, I used them right away in my simmering pot.

Now, you could use any cooking vessel for your simmering pot. Maybe an old canner from the Salvation Army. Just make sure your pot is big and will fit well on the back of your stove, and that it won't easily boil dry. You don't want to start a fire ... like "ye ole gal." Just turn it off when you leave the kitchen after doing dishes or other chores. You could even take an old crock pot that you aren't using and put the spices in this for a humidifier. If you have little ones, make sure the pot is way away from them. If you have toddlers that climb on cabinets, forget this

Christmas idea.

But, ya know, when adding your old outdated herbs to your pot, just add stuff that would go together. Like part of a bottle of basil would go with an old bottle of onion or garlic powder. If it is stuck in the bottom of the bottle, just add water to it and it will come out. Or you could put in some old black pepper or paprika. I love the smell of onions, garlic and basil together. Smells like an old Italian home where Mama is making her famous spaghetti sauce. Or you could put in orange peels and other citrus fruit peels, and add the old bottles of ginger or nutmeg or cloves and cinnamon. And, for cryin' out loud, the spices at the Family Dollar store are only two for a buck, and those spices are nice and fresh (or a whole lot fresher than what ya got in your spice shelf that are years old.) Just start out with fresh spices this year for your Christmas baking.

Ya know, lately, I have been hunting for the cinnamon sticks and can't find them cheap. Haven't found any to put in tea.

Speaking of tea ... I used to let my children make tea and stir it with a candy cane, for

Christmas. Or the cocoa mix can be served to the children with a candy cane in it. Candy canes are so cheap at the stores, too. We often decorated the tree with them. My children all loved candy canes and would beg all Christmas season to eat them off the tree. We would let them. Heck, you are only a kid once. I know this is a lot of sugar for children, but I didn't feed my children a lot of sugar except at Christmas or other holidays. And they were all hyper, anyway, and it never hurt them any.

Well, I had better get to practicing what I preach and get to my home duties.

One other thing I wanted to tell you is that usually each year ... well, in the fall ... I buy an amaryllis flower to watch grow in the house. It blooms about Christmas time if you plant it in the fall. But you could get one, even now, and start it and it would be about ready for the New Years. I have a red one this year and it is just starting to barely come out. It will be in full bloom for Christmas. I only paid three bucks for it, and oh! it gives the family such joy to watch it grow. The stalk is over a foot high and the blooms will be huge.

Dear Christmas Mothers

6
An Old Fashioned Home

December 17, 2003

I just put my turkey in the oven for our dinner tonight.

I was sitting in the living room and looking at the low and sweet Christmas lights. What an old fashioned Christmas home!

The presents under the tree are humble, but there, and wrapped awaiting the looks of surprises upon our children's faces. Just little things that say, "We love you, kids. Merry Christmas." Of course, we already exchanged Christmas gifts with the older children at Thanksgiving.

Yesterday, as we came home from shopping, I could smell the stew cooking in the crockpot, even on the front steps outside. It's no wonder it drew Danny home. But that is what an old-fashioned Christmas home is to smell like ... food cooking and folks laughing and giving to each

Dear Christmas Mothers

other humble gifts. It's the spirit of giving and joy.

This morning, I put my crock pot back in place with a little beef stew left. I have added a can of mixed vegetables and some beef gravy mix. It will make a light soup to eat for lunch with crackers and cheese.

The crock pot meals are such helpers for me around the Christmas season. To make the stew, I just put in some partly cooked hamburger, then some onions and carrots and potatoes. (I leave the onion whole, as Papa and his seeds are onion haters. They like the taste but wouldn't want to eat one.) Anyway, I put in some cabbage, too. Then I added a can of diced tomatoes and a can of tomato soup, and a beef gravy mix from Aldis. Then just add some water ... ya can't go wrong. Put in salt and black pepper.

Then, when the stew is about all gone, you can add some cans of vegetables and water and make a nice light beefy soup. After it boils, I will add some broken up spaghetti. I like to have soup out in case Dan or David stop by, or Mary. This way, I can visit and feed the company at the same

Dear Christmas Mothers

time.

One thing I do, too, is this. At the end of the day, I just take the whole crock pot out and put it in a cold place, like the fridge or the porch. Then, the next day, after I have had stew, I just bring the crock pot pan in again, put it back in the crock pot thing, turn it back on, and add the cans of vegetables, etc. to make a light soup. It's easy and keeps things movin' around here. Papa is honestly always hungry, so this keeps him happy.

And, ya know, too, I want to say that … Boy, how can I say this? I didn't always have a happy season at Christmas. I had to stay up alone on Christmas Eve and put toys together by myself. But I did because I lived from my visions from within my heart. The ones God gave me for a restored family, ya know? And now you can imagine why, as I look around me, in a safe and warm Christmas nest … my eyes pour out tears of gratitude to my Lord Jesus Christ.

The Lord gave me a "new" husband, one who cares about me and my children. He gave me exceedingly and abundantly more than I could think or ask. He really did, and I praise Him for it. Out of the first twelve years of my marriage, I think Papa and I were together only a few years at Christmas. It made me very sorrowful and yet, I had children who needed to have a Christmas, and I made one for them. I had to live by the promises of God and nothing less. And He did not forsake me, and He made it all up to me a hundred times over.

I wonder if this is His presence I sense this morning, as the house seems like His manger, lowly and quiet and silent with love.

7
Home Made Candles

December 1, 2003

I had this big, dark green candle. I didn't really like it, so I melted it down for the wax, making sure I kept the candle part with the wick in the center whole. So it went from a fat candle to a skinny one. I made one candle by putting it in a quart jar. The other half, I put in a little round enamel pan red and white ... it is a really old pan ... chipped ... I had gotten it at a garage sale. It's probably 1930s? So, while the candle was soft and in the pan, I put pine cones around it, and over the pine cones, I sprinkled whole rosemary and whole cloves. I had dried some of the tiny red hot peppers this summer, and I put those around the pine cones for color. It made the sweetest old fashioned winter candle and it really smells good, too. When Papa got home from work, he saw it and really liked it. It looks very woodsy and back to the land.

Dear Christmas Mothers

Also last evening, before Jim got home from work and had supper, I changed my big table. We have two leaves in our table because of all the family being here. But I will leave it large for Christmas, too. Anyway, I took the Thanksgiving plastic cloth off and put on a pretty old-fashioned Christmas tablecloth, plastic and pretty. It looks a little like the Mary Ingelbert designs. My table now would seat ten, so it's a long tablecloth.

I get my tablecloths for a song. I only pay about three bucks for them. I get them at the Dollar Stores or wherever. I have to cover my big table in plastic because I use it to work on. My kitchen doesn't have the counter space, or much space of any kind, so I use my big table to roll out pies and noodles and cookie dough. I use it to do my crafts on and canning, etc. I would be lost without my big table. But I do keep it well covered in at least a couple layers of tablecloths.

Last night, I decorated my table. I put my old fashioned candles on it that I had just made. Then a basket of napkins and, also, a rooster cookie jar that I use for crackers. He is sitting

Dear Christmas Mothers

there all proud of himself. But his dark red comb was needed to add a Christmas red to my table. Papa had bought some oranges and bananas and I put them in an old red and white bowl and set them on the table. (Always, the old fashioned families had oranges at Christmas.)

For my paper Christmas napkins, this is what I do. I buy cheap white paper napkins and then some pretty Christmas napkins. I put out just a few of the Christmas napkins and use mostly the white ones. It's too expensive to use the Christmas napkins all through the season. For Papa's meals, I give him a nice napkin, and for company. But my kids come in and see napkins on the table and use them for everything. But I can make a nice package of Christmas napkins last for the whole season. Also, I bought the plain red napkins at a sale some place ... can't remember now ... but I will use them, too, if I need to — if I run out.

I like to have things out on the table in case Papa wants a snack or whatever. I always have a tall cup of spoons on the table, too. One item I always have on my table is my little sugar bowl.

Dear Christmas Mothers

It is an enamel blue and white speckled little pot with a lid and bale handle. It looks really old-fashioned and woodsy.

My son John really drew me out when he was home. He admires the old time ways within me and seems to call me out. Both he and his wife Christine do this to me. John remembers me this way as he was growing up. John's drawing this out of me is such a gift given to Mother from her children. He held an old treasure in his heart and drew it out as he said, *"Mom, remember?"*

8
A Hand Made Christmas
December 16, 2002

You know what, Christmas Mothers? Children don't know that you are poor unless you tell them. Some years, we had so very little money to spend at Christmas, and some years, we had more. But you know, if you just have a little gift for the children to open up under the tree, that is enough.

We mothers used to mainly make our Christmas with our hands. I would make the cut out cookies galore. They are so simple to make with just the most basic ingredients, and then I would frost them with simple butter frosting. Just melt some margarine in a pan and add a bit of milk, and then start adding powdered sugar until it is thick. Add a bit of vanilla if you have it. I would frost the cookies and then sprinkle colored sugar over the top.

I made my colored sugar with food coloring.

Just put some sugar in a cup and add the food coloring and mix it up. Beet juice could be used to color sugar, just a little bit ... it will turn out an old fashioned red. Making the colored sugar with the plain white crystal sugar makes the cookies look so much more old fashioned and pretty. If you have some kool-aid, you could mix it with a drop of water and color your sugar with that. Just put about a half cup of sugar in a bowl and put the coloring in, just a drop, and then it will dry pretty fast. I save mine, too, until I decorate again.

I have the old Amish mother and father cookie cutters. Mary has made so many cookies with these and decorated with maybe 3 different kinds of sugar on each cookie. Just smooth it on with your fingers. We haven't made any cookies yet. I have been making other things.

You can just take an afternoon and make cookies with the children. They would love that. Tell them that this is their Christmas and that they can make their own cookies. We used to always save our coffee cans and decorate them with Christmas paper, and then we would put

Dear Christmas Mothers

cookies in them. Maybe the children could decorate their own containers and put their own cookies in them. It's a simple project. I used to cut a brown paper sack, lay it out flat, and then wad it up so it would look old, then cover my can with this. Then I would tie a brown string around it. Maybe the children could color on the paper that covers their cans. And then maybe you could make special cookies for them to open on Christmas morning, too.

You know, the old time Mothers never bought much for the family for Christmas. It was mainly handmade things. And their Christmases were so beautiful.

I think a mother who can set a festive Christmas table is worth her weight in gold. To just put a candle on the table and light it, and just make it pretty. My grandma Jaunita used to use her red and white linens at Christmas. She didn't have fancy tablecloths with a Christmas design, but she would just use a tablecloth that had red and white flowers on it. Oh, she would set a beautiful table. So many of us have dishes that we never use. Let's get them out and use them this Christmas. I have a lovely set, white with red roses on them. I must get them out tomorrow. Papa has a box under the tree for me. I know it is a set of Christmas dishes. The children and their Daddy always know what to buy Mama ... "dishes." Danny, last year, got me dessert plates at the dollar store for a buck each ... the Currier and Ives, each with a different winter scene on them.

Also, I left my big table out with the two leaves in it from Thanksgiving. This way, I have fixed a place at the end for us to eat our meals, and the other end I use for baking. I have my white poinsettias in the middle. I don't have the counter space, so I just make a space to mix my sausage and to do other kitchen chores at the end of the table. I made a second batch of sausage this afternoon. I have to knead it on the table. I will give some of this away for Christmas.

I try to have my cassette recorder out and the Christmas songs playing, and the candles lit on the table as I cook and make things for Christmas. I think that Mother brings in the Christmas spirit to the family. We need so much

Dear Christmas Mothers

to make a shelter for family, and the Christmas season is the time to do it.

One year, I had a lot of cranberries in my freezer and strawberries, too. I made the cranberries as usual, as the directions said. Then I added the strawberries and mixed them up, adding sugar until I thought it was good and tasty. The cranberries thickened the strawberries and it made a wonderful jam. I called it Christmas Jam. I put it in jars and gave it away for Christmas. As long as you have the cranberries to thicken the jam, you could use red raspberries or apples to make your jam, and even apricots. Oh, yum, that sounds so good!

Dear Christmas Mothers

9
Christmas Fudge

December 10, 2004

I think today I will make my Christmas Fudge.
It is called EASY Fudge or "Never Fail Fudge."
The recipe is on the back of the marshmallow
cream jar. I make it once a year at Christmas and
it makes a lot. I mean, if you go to buy the fudge
at the mall, it costs plenty. But this recipe on the
marshmallow cream jar is just as good and rich
and sure a lot fresher ... and it makes 3 pounds.
That is a lot of rich Christmas Chocolate.

I sometimes buy a can of mixed nuts and put
this into my candy. But you may just want to use
peanuts or walnuts or pecans. I don't crush the
nuts up; I leave them whole. And when you cut
the fudge you cut right through the nuts. It's a
nice clean cut. But, anyway, I won't write out the
recipe because if you plan to make this fudge,
you need the marshmallow cream, anyway, and
the recipe is on the back of the jar. I just dug

Dear Christmas Mothers

around in my freezer and found some fresh walnuts in a bag, so I will use walnuts to make our Christmas Fudge.

In the old days, I used to buy a jar of marshmallow cream at Christmas and, if I didn't hide it right away, Dan and David and the boys would all get into it and try to eat it. So when I would go to make my fudge, the marshmallow cream would be half eaten. So if ya think about it, when ya go to the store to get the marshmallow cream, if it's on sale, buy two. One for the fudge and one for the kids to sneak into.

A nice thing to do with your Christmas Fudge after you make it? Well, you can go to the Salvation Army and get the most lovely Christmas tins. I just take mine home and wash them out real good. And then I line mine with the light tissue paper that is a buck for about 10 big pieces ... it's beautiful paper and I would have died for it in the 70s. But, anyway, line your tin with the tissue, and then put a layer of plastic wrap over the tissue so the candy won't melt through. But this makes a nice candy box to put on the table for the holidays. And, of course, this

Dear Christmas Mothers

recipe makes 3 pounds of candy. You could give some of this fudge away for a Christmas gift, wrapped in pretty Christmas tissue and a nice Christmas tin. We used to do this and, oh folks, love fudge for Christmas.

I buy a container of the old fashioned hard candy at Christmas. (Mary always loved to get into that when she was little.) It only costs 2 bucks at the Dollar Store for a big can. And, often, if I was giving fudge away for Christmas, I would sprinkle some of the hard candy in my tin along with the fudge to make it festive.

And you need a heavy pan to make your fudge. I love my old pan I got at the Salvation Army right after Thanksgiving ... the one with the big heavy red lid? The pot is black and is like a cross between a cast iron and an enamel. The red lid is enamel but very heavy, like cast iron. But I have had a ball with this pan ever since I got it. I have made lots of soup in it.,And it has a nice heavy bottom, and this will be perfect for candy makin'.

You could use your heavy cast iron Dutch oven to make your fudge, too. I usually use mine each year. But this year, I am using my new pan, as it is a bit lighter. And I have to hold it and scrape the candy out at the same time. So a lighter pan will be easier to work with.

The kids get such a kick out of me when I show them my big pan with the red lid on my stove. I just think it is cute.

Also, when I got my last stove I got a small white stove, as my kitchen is so small. I call it my Minnie Mouse Stove, as my kitchen looks like Minnie Mouse cooks in it, anyway. But this little white stove reminds me of the 1920s stoves. The ovens in them were so small. But the Mothers cooked huge meals in them.

When Papa and me were first married, we had this apartment that had a huge kitchen. It was really old fashioned and I loved it. It had very little counter space, as the kitchen cupboards went from the ceiling to the floor. The ceilings were very high, of course, probably 10 ft high. You had to practically get a ladder to get into the highest cupboard. I didn't even use these cupboards, as I was just a young wife with barely any dishes anyway. But I filled up the lower cupboards.

Dear Christmas Mothers

Anyway, this kitchen had an old white stove in it from the 30s or 40s. The stove had 2 ovens in it with 2 thermostats. The small oven, you used for every day, and the big oven was for big family meals. But you could have 2 things goin' on at the same time, as each oven had its own temp control. I loved baking bread in the big oven and baking the family meal in the other side.

Happy Cookin'

Dear Christmas Mothers

10
A Christmas Homestead

December 6, 2004

Dear Christmas Mothers, Good morning. It's early morning on the Hultquist Homestead. It's another day for me to make a home here for Papa and for the older kids who run in and out. Dan was here last night with Suzy. Papa was at work. So Dan will be back this afternoon to visit with Jim. Late morning here, we will be putting up the Christmas tree. Today is Jim's day off so he will have a ball putting up decorations. I will probably make popcorn this afternoon after lunch.

When Dan came in last night, he said, "Oh, Mom, the house looks so pretty." Jim and I have cut branches of evergreen from our tree and put it all over the house. We put branches over the doorpost going to the kitchen and on the one to the upstairs. We made a wreath for the front door and I put branches of evergreen in the windows. To make the wreath, Papa just cut a bunch of branches about 2 feet long. And then I just gathered them all at the top and put a ribbon around it. We didn't make it round. Then I just stuck it on a nail on the door. You could put a wire around it if you wanted to and then twist a circle to make a loop to hang on a nail. Then I hung a strand of gold bells on it.

One thing I like to do with the branches is I like to soak them a bit in a bathtub of water. This way, it makes the branches easier to work with. They aren't so stiff and immovable. Also my branches will be up for a few weeks so I don't want them to dry out.

About 5 years ago, Jim planted a blue spruce in our back yard. It is so pretty and tall now. It grew quickly. So a few days ago, Papa just took his saw and cut the branches for the house from the bottom of the tree, so it doesn't ruin the beauty of the tree. When I decorate, I love to bring the outside in and then spruce it up a bit. We have tiny red bows that we put on the swags of evergreen. Well, except for the front door

Dear Christmas Mothers

evergreen. I have a bigger ribbon for that. Still, I keep the colors more subdued and old fashioned.

Danny wanted to go upstairs last night to borrow one of Jim's T-shirts. But he said, "Mom, I better not go upstairs, huh? Dad probably has Christmas presents up there." Oh, Danny Dee — at 22, still a hungry hearted little Christmas elf. We pick out funny things for the kids for Christmas. Well, Dan has needed a winter coat. He has one but — well? Well, anyway, Jim decided to give Dan his black leather motorcycle jacket. Jim doesn't drive a motorcycle but we had gotten this really nice black jacket with the zippers on the sleeves, etc. at a sale last summer. Well, Dan loves it. And for Christmas we are wrapping it up and putting it in a box for Dan. We will put in new gloves and a black scarf for his neck and some Elvis sunglasses. And then we have a card from last year that Brandon gave us. It's a big card with Elvis on the front? In the inside, it says, "I hope your Christmas rocks." Well, anyway we will take the picture and get a frame for it and put those in with the coat. Dan will love it. He thinks he is Elvis, ya know? And if ya look at the old pictures of Elvis, Dan does look like him. And, yes, our Christmas did Rock last year and I am sure it will this year, too. But I am glad that Dan is getting out of the Punk Rock. Thank God!

But, anyway, it will be a fun day today as Papa will be off putting up the tree. And Dan will come over and maybe some of the other kids. I may have Baby today — I don't know. I am going to bake this morning and make Christmas cookies and maybe some bread. I will make some Cheese Potato Soup. I will put some left over fried bacon in it that I saved in the refrigerator. Dan loves coffee so I will have the coffee on. I know coffee isn't that good for ya but, Christmas Sisters, things could be worse! I can't believe that some of you won't fix your husband's coffee?

And don't forget, Christmas Sisters, that a homestead just means a place where you have a home. Like a bedstead is a place for a bed. So you can call your home a Christmas Homestead, too, even if you live in a trailer or apartment.

I always decorate like I live in a cabin in the woods. Papa and me always get a real tree for

Christmas. Yes, it is a mess and, yes, Peggy Sue is just a kitten and will climb it and Jim will have a fit. And, yes, Baby Rose will get into it, too. But that's OK. Life is goin' on at the Hultquist Home and we wouldn't know what to do without some action, anyway. Papa had said a few years ago that we would just get a small artificial tree as the kids were all gone. But Mama insisted that we have a real tree. Then this year, I gave in and said, "OK, we can get a small tree." And Papa wouldn't hear of it and went out and bought one the same size we use every year. Well, that is fine with me. And I am letting Papa have a ball with it.

While I am the type to want the more subdued colors of nature, Papa loves the brightest he can get. Soooo — this year the tree is all his idea as I got to decorate with the evergreen in an old fashioned way. Papa is going to decorate the tree in the 50s style — the bright, hanging green and red Christmas ornaments? Oh, I hate those things! Metallic red and green and silver? But Papa will love it, and I will just wear sunglasses when I look at it.

Dear Christmas Mothers

And ya know, I know that Jesus is the reason for the season. But I don't try to hook Jesus in with this as an afterthought with Santa Claus. To me it's two different things. Jesus is my Lord. But ya know, I am dealing with folks around me that aren't all believers yet. Or they are young in the faith. And I can't make this holiday time a time for fighting and hell on earth. I use Christmas as a time to celebrate family and a time to show the ones I love a fun family time. And if Jesus wasn't my Lord, I couldn't even have the courage to do that.

I try to make a Joyful Holiday for my family out of a heart that sometimes wants to just roll over and play dead. It takes a lot of spiritual strength to make a Christmas for our families. I mean, especially if they aren't all saved. It's hard to look past the obvious things that just ain't right yet in the family and go on and be joy filled. And yet, as we Christmas Mothers make our holiday preparations, we walk by faith and not sight. We go on in God and make the holiday a Joy. Because one of these days when we least expect it, all will be well with all of our families. And won't we want to hear our children say about us, "Mama made a Christmas for all of us. Her heart must have been broken as she saw some of us living against what she taught us. But Mama walked in faith. Her and Daddy made a Christmas. An old fashioned Christmas that we can never forget."

We must remain strong, dear Sisters, in the face of adversity. We must remain the stars of our homes. The light that shines brighter than the Christmas lights.

Let us this Christmas season

light our kitchens with

Love, Forgiveness and Hope.

Let's keep our visions crisp and clear.

May our faces shine with the anointing

of Jesus Christ.

As servants of Christ

let's make our homes Christmas homes of Joy.

11

Cocoa Mix

December 3, 2004

You need a big gallon jar to make this mix. Or just make it in a big bowl or a sack* and then distribute it into other containers. But this mix will last a big family the whole winter, well past Christmas.

Ok, put in your bowl:

7 and a half cups of instant milk.

Add:

2 cups of sugar

1 cup of cocoa

one fourth teaspoon of salt.

Now mix this up really good and you got it, Darlin'. Use a third cup of mix for a mug of hot water.

Now, of course you could add less instant milk and add a container of the instant dry cream. Or add brown sugar instead of white, or use powdered sugar. You could add a can of Hershey's Cocoa Mix to this, too. But, if you are poor, you can just make it simple like my recipe.

And it's ok to be poor. It ain't a sin — it's just uncomfortable. You won't have the same kick in your cocoa as your rich friends but you will be thinner, and for this, you can smile smugly. And, actually, you could laugh out loud when no one else is around.

But you must never, ever complain that you don't have the money to buy the dry cream or the Hershey's Cocoa Mix. Never let the rich ladies see you sweat ... as they don't know that you have to make your Christmas Cocoa Mix with just cocoa and instant milk and plain table sugar with a pinch of salt. Of course you can't afford a vanilla bean that costs 3 dollars! But add instant vanilla pudding and fake it, and smile big like you have a vanilla bean in your Cocoa Mix but somehow it just dissolved. Hhmmph!!! Never let the devil see ya sweat. Or Jezebel, who couldn't make a biscuit if her life depended on it.

Ya know, Dixie used to tell me a story. It was

about this husband who was always drunk. At one point, he got full of whiskey and shot up the town with his shot gun. His wife was a saint and prayin' for her wayward husband. When someone asked her about her husband shooting all the street lights out, she said, "Well, he is a pretty good shot for being so drunk." This woman never let the devil see her sweat. And ya know what? That woman's husband got saved because his wife wouldn't give up prayin' for him. And that's all it takes, simply, is prayer.

We ain't supernatural. We can't make things happen. But we can stand with our arms raised up like Moses so that God can defeat the army against us. Just stand, dear saints, with arms lifted to Jesus, for in Him comes your help. Stand up in His glory. Having done all to "Stand." Stand in Him and, when your arms feel tired, let the saints come along and help you hold up your arms of faith. But don't put 'em down, dear Mothers and wives. If ya don't give up, you will see His glory.

*Put 2 paper grocery sacks together to make it strong. Then roll down the top of the sack to make a bowl. Roll about half way down.

12

Homemade Christmas

December 2, 2004

Dear Wise Christmas Sisters, Yesterday, Papa and me went to the Dollar Store, and I got so many cute things. I put way more in my shopping basket than what I need. Then, just before I got to the check out, I put a bunch of stuff back. I will say about candy and crackers, "Oh, I don't need them I can make them." And I will look over my cart and think of what I can make at home and not buy.

I used to make crackers out of left over bread dough. Just roll out the bread dough really thin and then cut it in squares with a pizza cutter. Then prick holes in the squares and salt them or put Parmesan cheese over the top, and bake them like cookies. You could put garlic and pepper on them. But the old time Mothers never bought crackers ... they made them.

And I used to make bread sticks a lot to use with soup. Just take your bread dough and flatten it on a pan and let it rise about 15 minutes ... not long. Then just cut strips with your pizza cutter. I would fix these plain and then, when they came out of the oven, I would butter them and put Parmesan cheese on 'em. Our children would eat these as they played outside on winter evenings after supper. They would run in the house, "Mom, can I bring out bread sticks for Nathan and Tiffany?" (neighbor children.) I would say "Sure, I have plenty." And my bread sticks were big and fat and, when you ate one, you got filled up.

Anytime I made bread, I made a lot of dough and made bread rolls, cinnamon rolls, and a few loaves of bread. At Christmas, I would take my bread dough and make 3 long strands of bread. I would sugar and spice the long ropes with cinnamon and brown sugar and butter. Then I would braid the pieces. Sometimes, I would put the braided dough on a long cookie sheet and then flatten it so it would be wide, then let it rise and bake it. After it was done, I would decorate

Dear Christmas Mothers

the bread. Sometimes, I would sprinkle on homemade green sugar. But then sometimes, I would put some butter frosting on it and color this green. Then I would take the maraschino cherries, slice them in half, and put them on the bread. And then put pecans on it, like every other one. Pecan and then cherry, etc., down the center of the loaf. If ya just used a package of pecans sparingly, and the cherries, you can make a lot of Christmas bread with them. Then sometimes I would make the cinnamon braid and I would put it in a circle and bake it like that, in a round pan. Or make a circle with the dough and put it on a large cookie sheet and it will turn out like a Christmas wreath. And then just decorate it like a Christmas Wreath.

You could even use the frozen bread dough for some of this until you felt sure enough of yourself to make your own. But a bread machine, I think, would interrupt my creativity. But, ya know, with a big family I would just make up a big bunch of bread dough and make things for Christmas. And we always give Christmas bread to the neighbors. To use the frozen bread dough, just put your loaf out on the cupboard and let it soften, and then slice it length wise in thirds. Then butter it and put the cinnamon on it and the brown or white sugar. Then braid it up tight and put it in a loaf pan and let it rise, and bake it. When it is done and cooled, you could frost it with butter frosting. White frosting with colored sugar on the top looks "Christmasy." Or stick nuts and cherries on the top of the bread, down in the frosting, so it will stick good.

Butter Frosting: Just take a stick of butter, put it in your sauce pan, and melt it. Put in about a fourth cup of milk. Then, just add as much powdered sugar as ya need to make a thick frosting. (I have never used a recipe for this — sorry.) But then, at the end, just put in vanilla. There were years, back raising the children, that I would run out of powdered sugar. So I would use half powdered sugar and half flour. I really like it better with using half flour. Ya have to keep stirring when ya use the flour and let it thicken.

And, ya know, I couldn't afford all the sugars when we had all the kids home. Often, I would make the powdered sugar with putting plain table sugar in my blender with a bit of white flour, and then just blend it up. This makes a nice powdered sugar, and often I would add molasses to my white sugar to make brown sugar. Heck, if I got white sugar and plenty of it for baking, I was cookin' on all 4 burners, huh?

But I always just made up my mind that my children would not have lean Christmases, as long as I could buy flour and lard and sugar. I mean, I would not confess negative over my Home Christmas. If the children would ask to invite the neighbor children in for cocoa and treats, then I made the children welcome. My children were proud of Mama, that she made such good holiday treats. And, of course, many of the neighbor children had never tasted a homemade cookie, and they loved my baked goods. I would just try to be gracious and kind hearted and enjoy the children.

But, ya know, I would just get busy and make a Christmas. Papa would haul in a big 50 pound bag of white flour on his shoulder and I would make Christmas out of it. Papa would carry it in

Dear Christmas Mothers

at Christmas and slam it on the table like it was fresh meat, and he would say, "There ya go, woman … ya got flour." And with some meat and some potatoes and vegetables, we raised 6 children, and always had a Merry Christmas.

And I never started baking for Christmas unless I had a pot of homemade soup bubbling on the stove. Even if I started early morning, I had to have soup on the stove. Because once I got going on the baking, I didn't want to stop and make dinner. So the older kids could serve their own soup and fix some for the little ones while I baked. It is a common sight to see spilled soup on my table, mixed with flour. Because I never baked without making soup first. And then I would make the bread dough as the soup simmered. Then the first part of the dough I would make pan rolls. I would just take the dough before it rose and put it on my baking sheet and cut it like a cake? Then I just had this to rise once and I baked it, and it was ready for the family for lunch … just pan rolls.

But I was not a stingy mother who was always yelling out, "Don't eat that! We won't have enough." My children were all thin, and still are, but I always made sure that my children were well fed. I didn't want them to get sick, as we couldn't afford a doctor. So they had plenty of fresh fruit and vegetables, and much homemade vegetable soups and stews. I didn't think about vitamins; I thought about having a wholesome homemade home to raise my babies in. I thought of their souls and their comfort.

I always had the coffee on for Papa ... he needed it ... it was a comfort to him, and especially at Christmas, with a piece of cherry pie. A cup of coffee is very comforting to a man, and a hot supper.

A wise Mother builds her house, and especially at Christmas time.

Make a homemade Christmas for your dear Families ... don't think about going to the store first. Go through the pantry cupboards and look at what you have. Do you have some hamburger, and some potatoes and vegetables? Fry up some meat with some onions and fresh pepper and salt. This is the smell of home and family. After the meat has cooked, just throw in some tomato

Dear Christmas Mothers

soup and start adding vegetables. Add water to cover the vegetables. Let this cook slowly on the stove, or bake it in a slow oven for a few hours.

Then, if you have no flour or sugar, at least you have lunch started, and you can make a quick trip to the store. But if you have flour and sugar, just stay home and start making Christmas.

If you have to go out, here is a list of things you may need:

1. Well, first off make sure you have plenty of flour and sugar, and shortening or lard.

2. I always have cocoa in my cupboard.

3. Do you have cinnamon? For winter, I often fix a shaker of cinnamon and sugar for the table or to put next to the stove to cook with.

4. And, even now, as the children are grown, I still have a huge box of instant milk that I cook with. Baby Rose drinks a lot of fresh whole milk, so I sometimes run out of milk and the instant milk is very handy to have to cook and bake with. And God knows I NEVER measure instant milk. To make gravy or to bake with, just throw some

dry milk in, and add water until it looks right. If I had to measure stuff all the time, I would be as crazy as a Loon. Not to mention, I wouldn't get anything else done.

5. Well, ya need eggs ...do ya have some? No? Well, write it down on your list.

6. Ya got chocolate chips? If you can afford them, be sure to get some for the Christmas Chocolate Chip Cookies. And, heck, you don't need to put a whole package in your recipe. Just use a fourth of a bag per recipe. Jill R., if she ran out, would just put one chocolate chip on each cookie. Her kids couldn't wait to eat to the middle of the cookie to get the chocolate chip. She could make a package of chocolate chips last for months. If the cookies had just one chocolate chip in them, they were "Chocolate Chip Cookies," by golly, and no one complained. If you are poor, its legal to B.S. your kids. (That's the law, I think.) But, ya know, if Mama is ok, then all is well at the house.

7. Hey, and don't forget to buy coffee at the store for Papa and the neighbors who stop by for a Christmas visit.

8. And, ya know, if ya plan to make Cocoa Mix

Dear Christmas Mothers

for the holidays, don't forget the instant milk. I used to make ours with just the instant milk and sugar and cocoa. I mean, if you have the money, it's nice to buy the instant coffee cream to put in it, or a can of the cocoa drink powder, but ya don't need it. The kids won't know the difference, anyway. Be sure to put your cocoa mix in a big fancy jar, or even a coffee can, decorated with old-fashioned Christmas paper and a brown string. Put a third cup measuring cup down in the mix, so the kids know how much to use. And, if you are rich, buy a vanilla bean to stick down in the dry mix. But, if ya ain't rich, buy a few packages of instant vanilla pudding mix to put in the Cocoa Mix. That makes it MMMM Good.

These are simple things to make, and it will keep you from running to the store all the time. Just fill your pantry with as much as you can so that you can feel free to make a homemade Christmas, and many pots of soups and stews.

13

Cherry Kolaches and Hot Soup

December 20, 2004

Oh! My Dear Husband has been out workin' all day today. The temperature is in the single digits and, when it gets cold in Iowa, then, Baby, it is cold! I have made him a nice hot vegetable soup to come home to. Also, some dinner rolls and some Kolaches for dessert, and, of course, I have the coffee on.

Now, to make the Kolaches, all you do is make up your favorite sweet roll dough. You shape rolls like dinner rolls, round, and about 9 rolls in a square pan. Then, after they have risen, you make a good dent in them in the middle. In the dent, I put cherry pie filling, and I am baking them now. I put like 5 cherries in each roll. You push it down with a small teaspoon when you are putting the cherries in, so as to keep the dough punched down in the middle. After they are done baking, I will put powdered sugar on them. I

Dear Christmas Mothers

have them baking now, along with the dinner rolls. With one batch of roll dough, I made both the dinner rolls and the Kolaches.

Last night for supper, I took about a pound and a half of hamburger and flattened in a pan. When it had baked most of the way, I drained it; then I cut it in 4 serving squares and salt and peppered it. I put tomato soup on this with onions and carrots and pieces of celery. Anyway, I had a lot left over, so to make my soup today, I cut the meat all up in bite size squares and made soup with it. I have had it in the oven for hours and, oh, it smells good. I put more tomato soup in it and cut up potatoes and carrots. Also, corn, green beans, tomatoes and green pepper.

I had frozen some of my tomatoes in my garden this fall. I just put them in plastic bags and keep 'em in the freezer. Then, when I need some, I just take them out and drop them in the soup. I had also frozen green peppers, and orange and red. They freeze well and are so handy for winter soups and stews.

Anyway, I have been alone all day and had a lot of time to pray and get my bearings. But now, I am feeling lonely for Papa to get home and to eat supper with me.

Dear Christmas Mothers

14

Eggnog

December 31, 2005

When the children were young, we used to always buy a quart of eggnog at Christmas. Then I would put a quart of whole milk in it. We didn't like it so sweet, and mixing it made it last longer. I still mix mine when I get it. I got it out at Christmas but the kids didn't drink it that much. They just drank plain milk.

Anyway, I have had a lot of leftover eggnog and wanted to tell you some things you can do with it. You can make French toast with it. I just put the eggnog in a low flat bowl, add an egg, and beat it with a fork. If it's too thick, just add more plain milk. This makes a nice breakfast. Also, you can add it to your coffee if you like it like that. Or to hot chocolate. I have made many custard pies with leftover eggnog.

Jill makes eggnog bread. You could make

Dear Christmas Mothers

muffins using the eggnog, rather than just plain milk. I have made a lot of bread pudding with it, too. You can use it for about any baking that you use sugar in. Just substitute the liquid for eggnog. You could make pancakes, too. The eggnog is just milk and cream, eggs and sugar, and spices and vanilla. So you can use it for cookies or cakes or whatever.

Custard pie is very easy to make. Old fashioned pumpkin pie is a custard pie. I have made pumpkin pie with eggnog before and it's good. But a custard pie is a pie that is made from eggs and sugar, milk and spices. The milk sets up in the custard because of the eggs. I have made many custard pies and so don't go by a recipe. But it would be, like, for one pie about 2 cups of milk and about 3 eggs and about a half cup of sugar and some spices. Throw in some vanilla and beat it up. I just make it and if it don't look right, I add things. But the old fashioned raisin pies were made like this, only with about about a cup of raisins in it and cinnamon. Sour cream raisin pie is good. But I used to use fresh raw milk and so had the real sour cream. I don't know how it would do with the sour cream from the store.

But with any of my writing, be sure to look up a recipe. Jim's mother just cooked from whatever wasn't tied down. And I learned to cook that way, too. Sorry.

15

A Joyous Christmas

December 21, 2005

Dear Christmas Sisters, Oh! Yesterday afternoon my friend Jill, who I often write about, and her husband Jerry came to our home to wish us a Merry Christmas! Oh, we had a jolly time. Jill and Jerry brought many presents and we had so much fun. Jill had made candy. On a lovely Christmas plate, she laid the dark fudge with walnuts Jerry had cracked. As a couple, they go out to the woods and find walnuts in the fall. Also, Jill brought a delicious pumpkin bread with the walnuts in it. They also brought 4 different kinds of Christmas candy. The dark fudge, peanut butter fudge, toffee, and caramel peanut clusters.

I had made potato cheese soup and a hot spicy chili for our little Christmas party. Then we had coffee and, last but not least, we had the Cherry Raspberry Christmas Cordial. So anything that was funny, anyway, just got funnier. Jill and I serve our men hand and foot. Jill said, "Jim is still your king," as I served him his soup. Well, she is the same with Jerry.

We laughed and had a joyous time. And, oh mercy! Jill made a lot more too. I will tell you about it. She and Jerry made these dipped pretzels. Oh, I hope I can describe how cute these are. You get the long thick pretzels and dip the ends in almond bark and then nuts or the Christmas sprinkles. You dip them most of the way down so you can hold onto them at the bottom without getting sticky. Jill bundled them up in plastic wrap with a simple Christmas string gathered at each end. It's the cutest bundle of candy sticks you have ever seen. I want to eat one but I don't want to mess up how cute they are wrapped. Then, also, Jill brought me some red pepper candles and another cute pumpkin candle. Also, hand lotion and a bar of a Lavender Camay soap. Very fragrant. Oh, it smells lovely. And Jim and I got Jill and Jerry a Poinsettia

Christmas flower. Jim had bought eight of these flowers for Christmas and has given many away.

Oh, also Jill gave me some Christmas potpourri. I just opened it this morning and put it in this old fashioned homemade basket. I had pine cones in it on my old buffet. And Jill's potpourri, spread in the basket, makes it look all the more woodsy. The basket smells homey … like it should be deep in a forest cabin home at Christmas time!

But, oh, we laughed and had fun.   And Jill is just like a wind-up toy. So Jerry tells her to start winding down as it was almost time to leave. They had other presents to deliver to friends. Jerry looked so handsome at 74 years old. His curly, thick, pure white hair just glistened in the candlelight. And Jill, as pretty and brown eyed and full of sparkle as ever. Watching Jerry and Jill across the table is entertainment enough, without any presents.

As Jill paused at the door and looked at the house one more time, just before our last goodbyes and hugs, she said, "Well, Connie, you talk about my house having the presence of the

Lord in it. Yours does, too." I looked at the house after she left and tried to see what she saw.

Old familiar friends are such a blessing at Christmas. As iron sharpens iron, old familiar friends sharpen our inner man. We find a stream of still living water in our wilderness. It washes us of the dust and dirt of the world, and refreshes and restores us at Christmas time.

This morning, I got an email from a friend of many years. She said that she and her husband wouldn't be celebrating Christmas that much. Just going to stay home, as it is such a sad time of the year. What with all the sadness in the world, who would feel like celebrating Christmas? Well, I know her husband to be full of fun and could kid a grasshopper into a belly laugh. I thought of him and how sad he must feel about his wife not making a Christmas for the family.

I know there is so much sadness in the world. I see it very keenly, too. But we as wives are not to take on the burdens of the world. We have homes to be keepers in. And when our families see others having a happy Christmas, then they

Dear Christmas Mothers

want to have fun and joy, too.

The Mothers in the Depression times had many parties and celebrations. Families gathered at the family home and brought homemade Christmas breads and cakes. They barely had the staples to cook with. They had ration stamps because of the war. So the old time Mothers would save up their ration stamps for a few months to make sure they had plenty of sugar for Christmas baking. The government gave out boxes of raisins to poor people and often the mother used raisins in a recipe to make it sweet.

Dear Sisters, as the times get harder, the Mother's heart should get merrier. There is strength in Joy. When the family sees Mother in her Christmas apron, rolling out and baking cookies, they, too, take heart. Mother's faith shines like a shooting star in the middle of the darkness around us. Her smile and her sparkle is water to a dry and parched soul.

Jill has brought me Christmas candy for 30 years. And she first started making it all when her husband left her. She made sure that she had a Christmas for her children in the midst of

Dear Christmas Mothers

much heartache. She was abandoned by her husband. But she made the most lovely Christmas home that anyone could imagine. She had food stamps, as she was determined to stay home with her children and care for them. She told the welfare board that she wasn't looking for a job. She told them her children had been abandoned and she wasn't going to leave them, too. And her little boy thought they were rich, as his mother always made such wonderful meals and crafts at Christmas. On the coffee table always laid shutoff notices for the lights and water and gas. Jill hardly had the money to pay for these utilities. But her children didn't know that. It was Christmas time and mother made a lovely Christmas. Not with a lot of presents and expensive things. No, Jill made a Christmas with the Joy of the Lord.

We all got a lot of free government cheese, etc. We were embarrassed — sure we were. But we didn't let our kids know. They needed food and the peace of God upon their homes. They didn't need a stingy whiny mother telling them that if their Dad wasn't such a jerk, they would have a

Christmas. Well, children don't need that garbage. Things are hard enough without hammering the children about not having any food at Christmas. I mean, go get some free food at a church if ya have to. When ya bring it home and it is behind closed doors, the children won't know where it came from. For their sakes, make a happy Christmas.

The old time Mothers always made a Christmas. Maybe it was all homemade, but they made a joyful time. And sometimes a family would invite friends over for a dance. The family would move everything out of the living room and then roll up the carpet to make a place to dance. And folks brought their fiddles and played music to dance to. And in the dining room was a big table and folks brought food to share and eat together. The old time families made their own entertainment. And then, too, they had many church activities at Christmas. And all the children got presents.

Oh, the old time Mothers loved their Christmas cards, and they saved them all from year to year. They decorated the whole house with Christmas

Dear Christmas Mothers

cards. They put special cards in the kitchen, taped on the wall where they could look at them as they baked their Christmas cakes. And they taped some on the window in the living room or on the door. The cards meant so much to them. Sometimes they made homemade cards out of lace and ribbon and butcher paper from the meat market. Mother saved every bit of paper and string that came into the house.

And one year, when my children were young we hadn't had any snow. And it was getting near Christmas. So we made snow flakes and taped them on the window to pretend it was snowing. The children made many Christmas pictures and we hung them in nice places in the living room. Right on the wall in prominent places. I considered my children great artists. And they are to this day. We would take a blue piece of construction paper and put cotton on it for snow and for a snow man. Then we would put drops of Elmer's glue on the picture and put silver sprinkles on it for the snow falling.

One Christmas when the children were babies, I was feeling especially dry in my soul. So much

Dear Christmas Mothers

work to do and so little comfort. You know how it goes sometimes. Husband is working hard to keep the family in shoes and winter boots. And somehow Mother's needs go unnoticed. I had prayed and asked the Lord to restore my soul. I asked the Lord for a poinsettia flower to put on my table. I didn't know how I would get it. So I made a picture of it with the children's crayons and taped it on my window. I didn't want to ask Jim for it as I knew he was burdened enough at Christmas. So I didn't tell anyone about it, just Jesus.

Well, pretty soon, Poinsettia flowers began to come right out of the sky. My neighbor Trudy brought me one over and has for the past 10 years now. Jim found one on sale and got me one — it was gorgeous. He was working at a hotel and, on Christmas day, Jim brought me home about five poinsettias. After Christmas, I found white poinsettias on sale for a buck and I got one. My home was awash with gorgeous scarlet red and snow white poinsettias that year. And every year since that year, Wild Man has bought me, and others, poinsettias for Christmas.

16

It's Almost Christmas

December 5, 2005

Well, yesterday we hadn't planned to take Baby out — just from her house to ours — but Papa got to telling me about Menard's where he went to get the kerosene. He told me about all the Christmas things they had out. So I said, "Well, I will call Tiff and ask her to dress Baby really warm and then we could take her to Menard's (Big Hardware Store) to see the Christmas lights." So we ended up taking Baby to see the Christmas lights on the way home.

Oh, Papa is just a kid himself and loved showing Baby Girl all the dancing Santas and all the battery run toys that jingled and sang. We had a ball walking up and down the aisles. Our only purpose was to delight Baby. And, of course, she loved it all and is such a good little girl. She is just pure dessert to me and Jim.

Wild Man, of course, loves to sing, and he and I sang Christmas songs to Baby Rose in the car as we traveled back home. Jim loves all the old songs and knows all the words. He sings "Frosty the Snow Man" and Jingle Bells and "Ya better watch out Santa Claus is coming to town." And Jim is a master at singing the old time Christmas carols.

We taught our children all the old Christmas songs in homeschool, as we never wanted them to forget them. What with our country trying to forget Christmas. How sad! We sang songs like "Noel" and "Little Town of Bethlehem" and "Oh Come Let Us Adore Him." We love all the old time Christmas Carols. And Baby from the back seat makes requests. She will call out "Ten Monkeys on the Bed." Or "MacDonald's Farm" — Jim and I sing that and go through about 10 different farm animals.

Mary, our girl of 20 years old, tells me, "Mom, I am the only girl my age who knows all the classic shows like *Meet Me in St Louis, Annie get Your Gun*, and the other old-time Broadway shows that were made into movies." Jim has a wonderful voice to sing and loves to dance. We especially love the song "Rockin' Around the Christmas Tree."

When the children were little, we all sang these songs. I have a tape of them singing with Jim and me. I know where the tape is but my heart would bleed if I were to listen to it. We had so many happy days. But now the Lord has given me and Jim Baby Rose to sing Christmas to. And we have little Romeo who don't like kisses but loves us just as much as Rose does. We have a new generation to teach Jesus to. What a blessing to have a new little boy and girl to love, and especially at Christmas.

When I was a little slip of a girl, my dad loved Christmas. His folks had a big tape recorder. Now, this was back in the 50's. The tape recorder had the big round reels. Anyway, Dad's stepdad recorded me and Dad singing "Rudolf the Red Nosed Reindeer." Even at 4 years old, I was looking for truth and told my dad on the record that Rudolf's nose was brown, not red. Grandpa Babe made a tape of the recording into a record. I think I still have the record someplace. But my Dad used to say, "Christmas is for kids."

I think the love we show our children at Christmas is so important. We really felt it was so important to teach our children the old time Christmas songs about Jesus. "Angels From the Realms of Glory" is such a lovely song. I taught my children to play this on the piano in homeschool. I play so much by ear that it was hard for me to learn notes on the piano. But I learned enough to teach my children to play simple songs. We had a children's book of Christmas carols and I taught them out of this book. They could play "Silent Night" and many Christmas songs. And we would recite Christmas poetry. My children always had good literature to read. And I raised my children to know the Lord.

Oh, gosh, mothers what a journey of faith so many of us are on. We did our dang best and it seems it wasn't good enough. So many writers quit writing when the kids get old enough to move out of the house. The Mothers' hearts are so broken sometimes. But we just have to keep on goin'.

17

Mother's Ways

December 8, 2005

When I was a young mom, I would get the recipes from the extension office. I loved them and had a notebook of them. I think I still have that notebook and I am gonna look for it today. Ya know, back in the old days, when I was alone to raise my children, they had some little housewife magazines out on the newsstand. Anyway, the ladies would write into the magazines and tell about their crafts and sewing. Oh, how I envied these ladies so much. They would write in something like, "My name is Alice Woods and I live in Tulsa OK." Then she would go on and tell the date of her birthday and her

Dear Christmas Mothers

wedding anniversary date, etc. Then she would say, "I love to sew, cook, bake, and I have many hobbies." Then she would tell what she collected from other states, like salt and pepper shakers or postcards from around the world. Just junk, really, by today's standards. But these women were stay at home mothers and didn't think of going any place. They went to the grocery store once a week and shopping for clothes about once a month or so.

But my life, when I read these letters from these little magazines was a total disaster. Sometimes I went to the prison on the Salvation Army bus and had a life that sure didn't include collecting postcards or salt and pepper shakers. I mean, that was my fantasy, was to have a normal life and collect stuff. But it was so soothing for me to sit outside in the summer and read about housewives with happy lives. They would tell about their dogs and send in household tips and recipes. They loved houseplants and doodads like crazy. They would crochet doilies to put under each lamp in the living room.

The furniture stores would advertise a room

full of living room furniture for not very much. It would include two step end tables, a couch and a chair, and a coffee table. And this is what most of the ladies had in the living room. Then they would make a pretty embroidered scarf for the back of the chair and one for the two arm rests. This was to keep the chair clean and less worn. And these scarves were washed about once a month and were ironed and put back on the chairs. The children couldn't eat in the living room, as it was more of a formal area. The children could play with the toys in the living room, though. And, usually, you had a hardwood floor with an area rug. Wall to wall carpeting wasn't real popular until maybe the 1960's.

And the housewives would have knick- knack shelves. Today they call them dust collectors. But Mother would collect things like little ceramic dogs or cats, or little China figurines, or the little Hummel figures of children, or little ceramic tea pots, or whatever. So when Christmas or a birthday would come around, the children would buy their moms and grandmoms something to go in their collection. Of course, by today's

Dear Christmas Mothers

standards, this idea is very unsophisticated. But back in the old days, the mothers cherished their little collections and remembered each Christmas when what child picked out each knick- knack. They were just sweet remembrance. And the children could pick something out with their own money and surprise their Mothers. Of course, Mother's eyes would well up with tears, as she was so proud and happy that her little one had known her heart.

But, ya know, Mothers back then were just happy with what they got. As a young wife, I would sit and read the stories of these Mothers and I would think, "Wow, to just worry about salt and pepper shakers?" Of course, when Jim got saved, I did then collect sugar and creamer sets from second hand stores. BOY! I thought I was cookin' on all four burners then.

And when I was a little girl going to school, we always bought a Christmas present for our teacher. Often, it was a nice Christmas card with a pretty cloth Christmas hankie. And some of the mothers would tat around the hankie and then

Dear Christmas Mothers

crochet around the outside. Then they would starch the hankie and they were very pretty and a nice gift.

The Mothers would carry nice purses, usually black, and they called them pocketbooks. And in it would be a clean handkerchief, and maybe a tube of red lipstick, a compact with a mirror in it, and very few other things. Maybe a comb or a toy to keep the children happy at the doctor's office. When we kids were ready to go in some place and our faces had candy on them, Mom would wet her hankie with some spit and wash our faces off and slick our hair down a bit. But the Mothers didn't get new purses except if the old ones wore out. They got a new purse maybe every few years.

This year, I got a nice winter coat from the Salvation Army. It looks new and is a dark blue wool long coat. Whenever I wear it, I think of the old time mothers that would pray for a winter coat back in the Depression era. A nice wool coat like that would have been such a prize back then. There is a sweet motherly spirit on that coat and I love it just because of that. But, ya know, back in the old days, Mother put her family first and a winter coat for her was the last thing she thought of.

I say all of this to say that many women in our country, or that will read our website, love to hear the old time stories. I sure did when I was a young mom alone reading the housewife magazines. It gives the Mothers a place to dream and somehow touch base with reality.

Sometimes we need to go back to the old ways to get our stability. In this age of feminism, we have, as women, lost our direction. So we must go back to the bend in the road to a time when life made some sense. A place where Mother was the Star of her Home.

Now, in this day, as I write to Mothers and wives who are tossed and turned as I was as a young mom, I am glad I can somehow comfort you through my writings on housewifery. I never could have in my wildest dream thought God would ever use me to write about homemaking and housewifery. But God is a God of miracles. And He comes to bind up the broken hearted and to set the captive free. All things are possible to those who BELIEVE.

Dear Christmas Mothers

Connie's Kitchen
{Recipes}

Dear Christmas Mothers

Recipes

Index of Cooking Ideas

Dear Christmas Mothers

Pumpkin Bread

1 cup of melted shortening
3 cups of sugar
4 eggs
one can of pumpkin
a cup of water

   Just beat this all up. Then add:

3 and a half cups of flour
2 tsp of baking soda
1 tsp of salt
1 and a half tsp. baking powder
1 tsp cinnamon
1 tsp ground cloves
1 tsp nutmeg

   Mix it all up and put in your greased bread pans. Makes about two large loaves. Bake at 350 degrees for an hour or until done.

Sugar Cookies

In a big bowl, put in:

2/3 cup of softened butter
3/4 cup of sugar
1 tsp of baking powder
1 egg
1 Tbs of milk
1 tsp of vanilla
2 cups of flour

Using a hand mixer, stir up the cookie dough until it is well combined.

After it is combined, just work it into a ball. Put it in the refrigerator for about 30 minutes.

Preheat oven to 375 degrees.

Then flour a surface to work on, and roll out the dough using about half this dough at a time.

Get out your favorite Christmas cookie cutters and be sure to flour them good.

Just roll out the dough and cut out your cookies.

If you will be decorating with sugar, sprinkle the sugar on before you bake them.

 Make sure your baking pan is well greased or buttered.

 Bake for 5 minutes or more. They should be brown when you take them out of the oven.

Acknowledgements

We'd like to thank Lynetta Hamm and the "Happy Housewifery" team (those who work behind-the-scenes on the website and letter group).

Your help and encouragement, through the years, made this book possible.

God bless you, and may all your Christmases be very special!

For information about Connie and her writings, please visit the *Happy Housewifery* site:

http://happyhousewifery.com

Available now!

The Hultquist family Christmas on CD.

On page 96, Connie mentions a Christmas tape her family made. She and Jim and some of the children sang together by the piano. This rare recording was made nearly 20 years ago. We've found the tape and transferred it to a CD!

Order your copy from Amazon:

Christmas at Connie's - 1996 (The Home Recordings)

[Running time: 26 minutes]

The Legacy of Home Press

ASIN: B00JH25HXW

For More Titles from "The Legacy of Home Press," please visit us at:

http://thelegacyofhomepress.blogspot.com

Made in the USA
Columbia, SC
10 December 2019

84643574R00065